Dear Readers,

In this book you will meet a little boy whose greatest joy was learning. Reading books gave him many pleasant moments, and it also made his mind powerful.

Benjamin Banneker gained knowledge from reading, and when he grew up he gave knowledge to others with his writing. He was one of the greatest scientists in our country.

You too can read and learn, so that one day you can make our world a better place in which to live.

Your friend,

Garnet Jackson

BENJAMIN BANNEKER

Scientist

Written by Garnet Nelson Jackson
Illustrated by Rodney Pate

 MODERN CURRICULUM PRESS

Program Reviewers

Maureen Besst, Teacher
   Orange County Public Schools
   Orlando, Florida

Carol Brown, Director of Reading
   Freeport Schools
   Freeport, New York

Kanani Choy, Principal
   Clarendon Alternative School
   San Francisco, California

Barbara Jackson-Nash, Deputy Director
   Banneker-Douglass Museum
   Annapolis, Maryland

Minesa Taylor, Teacher
   Mayfair Elementary School
   East Cleveland, Ohio

MODERN CURRICULUM PRESS
13900 Prospect Road, Cleveland, Ohio 44136
Simon & Schuster • A Paramount Communications Company

Copyright © 1993 Modern Curriculum Press, Inc.

Library of Congress Catalog Card Number: 92-28799
ISBN 0-8136-5228-6 (Reinforced Binding)   ISBN 0-8136-5701-6 (Paperback)

Text Printed on Recycled Paper

When Benjamin was a small boy,
Everyone knew
That one day great things
This child would do.

He started asking questions
As soon as he could speak.
In wonderment forever,
Answers he would seek.

While others ran merrily
At school during recess,
"I'd rather read from my books,"
Young Benjamin would confess.

1, 2, 4, 7, 3, 8, 14, 21, 13, 22, 32, 43, 31, 44, 58, 73, 57, 74, ?

He loved to play with numbers.
To him, math was a game.
He made up arithmetic puzzles
For friends who felt the same.

He grew up at Bannaky's Springs
Where work preceded play.
After plowing and planting,
His thoughts ran deep one day.

A great idea he pondered,
With math and science on his mind.

To make a grand clock—
The first one of its kind.

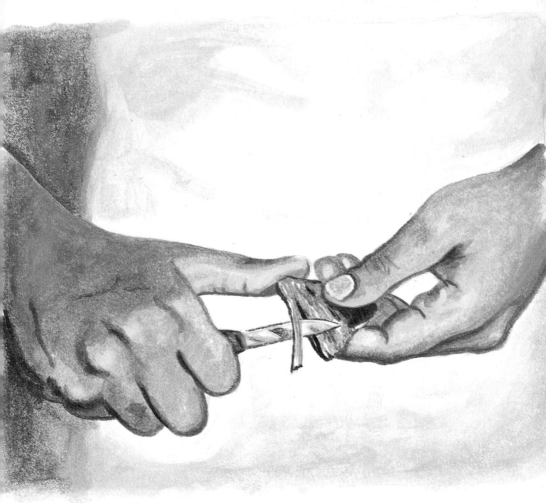

Benjamin chose his tools
And selected pieces of wood.
He carved barrel, wheels, and hands,
Making sure each part was good.

14

When he put the pieces together,
His clock kept perfect time.
Each hour, on the hour,
Mr. Banneker's clock would chime.

Quite a masterpiece
That all wanted to see—
Some say it was the first
In our fair country.

But Benjamin's thoughts moved onward.
New ideas he wanted to try.
With a telescope he'd borrowed,
Mr. Banneker studied the sky.

Benjamin wrote an almanac,
A book that brought him fame.
Scientists in America and Europe
Soon knew the Banneker name.

He also learned surveying—
That is, exactly measuring land.
The President asked him to help
When Washington, D.C., was planned.

Growing old at Bannaky's Springs,
Benjamin's hair turned silvery white.
As he was working, his clock was ticking
Throughout each day and night.

Mr. Banneker lived long ago,
And has been admired ever since.
What a great thinker was this grandson
Of an African prince!

Glossary

almanac (ôl´ mə nak´) A calendar for the coming year, with weather predictions, forecasts of the times for sunrise and sunset, advice for planting, and other information

barrel (bar´ əl) In a clock, the round case that holds the mainspring. As the mainspring unwinds, it turns the clock's wheels.

masterpiece (mas´ tər pēs) Anything done with very great skill

precede (pri sēd´) To go before

ponder (pän´ dər) To think deeply about something

survey (sər vā´) To measure the size and shape of a piece of land exactly, using special tools

telescope (tel´ ə skōp) A tool for making far-off things, such as stars, look closer and larger

About the Author

Garnet Jackson is an elementary teacher in Flint, Michigan, with a deep concern for developing a positive self-image in young African American students. After an unsuccessful search for materials about famous African Americans written on the level of early readers, Ms. Jackson filled the gap by producing a series of biographies herself. In addition to being a teacher, Ms. Jackson is a poet and a newspaper columnist. She has one son, Damon. She dedicates this book to the memory of her dear mother, Carrie Sherman.

About the Illustrator

Rodney Pate, a graduate of Pratt Institute, has worked as a commercial artist for ten years. He has illustrated over ten children's books, including *My Dad Is Really Something, Efan the Great,* and *My Body Is Private.* In *Benjamin Banneker,* Pate intertwines the deep, rich shades of oil paint and a creative use of shadows and highlights to capture the historic mood and relate the inner strength of the subject.